Keep on Moving

Keep on Moving

How to move through anxiety
and embrace the struggle.

JOHN WALSTON

*Keep On Moving: How to move through anxiety
and embrace the struggle*
Copyright © 2025 by John Walston

All rights reserved. No part of this book may be used or reproduced in any form, electronic or mechanical, including photocopying, recording, or scanning into any information storage and retrieval system, without written permission from the author except in the case of brief quotation embodied in critical articles and reviews.

COVER DESIGN BY Steve Teabout
BOOK DESIGN BY The Troy Book Makers

Printed in the United States of America

The Troy Book Makers • New York • thetroybookmakers.com

To order additional copies of this title, contact your favorite local bookstore or visit www.keeponmovement.org

ISBN: 978-1-61468-965-2

*This book is dedicated to everyone
fighting an invisible battle.
Keep fighting and know that we are
glad to have you here with us!*

Megan,

*Thank you for being the center of our universe.
You are the epitome of unconditional love
and commitment. I am blessed that you
are number one on my gratitude list.*

James,

*You taught me so much about overcoming anxiety
and life. Your kind soul, discipline and relentless
work ethic always inspires me to be a better person.*

Anna,

*You are my reminder that I can push through
anything and do it with a smile. Your ability
to be loving and a badass reminds me to be
relentless and pushes me to work harder.*

Mae,
*You are the old soul that reminds me
to be unique and fierce. Your words are powerful
and your heart is massive. You have taught me
that actions speak louder than words.*

Mom and Dad,
Love you!

Diane,
*Thank you for your guidance on this
writing journey. I appreciate your time,
your friendship and all your feedback.*

CONTENTS

Intro/Mission 1

1 · *Get Comfortable with Being Uncomfortable* 5

2 · *Cows and Buffalo* 15

3 · *You Are Amazing* 23

4 · *Inspire* 35

5 · *Movement is Anxiety's Kryptonite* 45

6 · *Resilience* 55

7 · *Be Where You Are* 67

8 · *Be Grateful* 78

9 · *Flip The Switch/Re-write Your Story* 89

RESOURCES

Re-writing Your Story 99

Recommended Reading 102

Recommended Podcasts 103

Keep On Movement- Join the Movement 103

INTRO/MISSION

There is a deep connection between physical movement and mental health. This book is a deeply personal look at how I was able to overcome mental health challenges and find clarity through movement. I wish you the ability to overcome your challenges and remind yourself to always Keep On Moving.

My wish for you is that you will find strength to believe in yourself. I want everyone to believe that they matter regardless of achievements or mistakes made. I want to encourage everyone to believe that they deserve to be loved. I want to encourage everyone to share their love with those around them. I want to spread a message that it is ok to not be ok and that your life is important.

I want you to know that each new day is the first day of the rest of your life regardless of what happened the day before or even years before. I want to encourage you to keep moving forward and never give up. I want to encourage others that harnessing the power within them is beautiful and worthwhile.

If you focus on solutions and do not get roadblocked by problems, then you can move forward in a productive direction. I have done this and in this book I will show you how.

There are several themes that seem consistent in the realm of "struggle" and challenges, whether the challenge is addiction, mental health, physical health, isolation, loneliness, shame, societal norms/assumptions, labels, etc… I want you to know that you are not alone. Human connection is a powerful medicine that we all need. The feelings of isolation and shame that result when we are going through a major struggle are real. We need to engage in honest conversations and ask tough questions to break down the barriers that create this isolation and shame. When I asked John Robinson, author of the book- *Get Off Your Knees,* how he would define resilience, he said, "Resilience is a commitment to being here for one more day. Get through the day and commit to getting up tomorrow to face the new day." If we can all commit to be here for one more day, then we give ourselves the opportunity to change the trajectory of our lives. Embracing the struggle is beautiful and is life changing.

Whether you are struggling with a physical health issue or a mental health issue, your struggle can be someone else's inspiration, and someone else's can be yours so find someone or something to inspire you. Celebrate your wins, even if it is as simple as getting out of bed and putting two feet on the ground. No matter if it takes you a minute or a week to shift your mindset, the goal is to keep moving forward. Giving up should not be an option. Movement is life, and if we are moving, then we will never give up.

You are capable. It does not require superpowers to change your life or to overcome a challenge. You are amazing and you possess all the powers to be an overcomer. Productive self-dialogue and focused effort will get you where you want to be. Even if you stumble, just keep moving forward and take action to push yourself in a beneficial direction. Even when you may not be able to change the situation around you, the solution to make yourself better is always available. Being an overcomer is one of the greatest achievements in life.

I had to learn this myself. I learned that instead of focusing on problems that could not be fixed right away, I could always work towards making myself better at managing the way I dealt with the problems. This realization is life changing and I want everyone to feel that incredible power which we are born with. Each day is a great day to be alive because it provides another opportunity to be better. That is the greatest blessing that we are given.

CHAPTER 1

Get Comfortable with Being Uncomfortable

"Pressure does two things- bursts pipes and creates diamonds. Which one are you?"

• • • BRIAN COOK • • •

How often do we shy away from the discomfort that could make us stronger? True growth rarely happens in comfort zones. In the Spring of 2018, I began to have hearing problems, tinnitus and balance issues. My doctor discovered that I had an Acoustic Neuroma which is a tumor that grows on the acoustic nerve. An acoustic neuroma is like hitting the lottery in the world of tumors because they are typically both benign and are slow growers. I was fortunate that my wife and I had time to assess and evaluate the situation before we needed to make decisions on treatment and a path forward.

The downside to the tumor was that I developed major anxiety during that time (I was never an anxious person) and running/exercise became my go to release for managing this new world of anxiety. The reality of my situation and the associated challenges that presented as a result of my acoustic neuroma were the source for my daily anxiety. As I researched more about the anxiety I was experiencing, it turns out that anxiety is a common emotional response to a vestibular disorder such as my tumor. After consulting with several doctors in the Northeast, my wife and I decided that surgery was my best option so that the tumor could be removed. I had surgery in Spring 2019 and I thought that this quick blip on the radar would be over and I would be able to move forward with my life. Post surgery, I lost my hearing in my left ear, the tinnitus was now louder, and my balance was not great, but I realized that my issues could all be managed and life should be back to a new normal soon. However, about 6 weeks after my surgery, my world exploded and I began a free-fall into a dark hole that I never would have imagined would become my life. Suddenly one night in May 2019 while getting ready for bed, I heard/felt a large "pop" in my head and immediately had massive tinnitus (like a giant fire alarm blaring in my head) as well as a constant echo where I heard everything inside my body reverberate in my head. My voice echoed like when you have a bad connection on the phone and you hear every word twice. Every step I took echoed in my head and the sound of every heartbeat in my chest echoed in my head. I did not know if I was having a brain aneurysm, a stroke, a brain hemorrhage or I was going to pass out and die soon. After a few hours, I did not die, so I could eliminate that possibility. I did not sleep all night and I just prayed that all the new crazy stuff in my head would go away in the morning. Unfortunately, all the craziness in my head did not go away. I called the doctor and he said "changes" in my head would be normal and I needed to be patient as there was still too much swelling in my head to see much on an MRI. I did not sleep for a few days, my anxiety was through the roof, and new psychotic feelings began to creep into my life. I had no control over what was happening in my head and I felt like I had no control of my life. The less control that I felt, the more I would go into a darker hole of emotional dysfunction. I was embarrassed to admit that thoughts of hurting other people or myself felt desirable because I was yearning for some control. I fantasized about wanting to take someone else's life and I hated myself for it. Additionally, it was exhausting each day trying to be as "normal" as possible when I was living in such a dark place.

My only release was to go outside for a run, and run so hard that I would push myself to physical exhaustion. It was the only relief that pulled me back from the darkness that had become my new life. I would run at all hours of the day and night. I yearned for the physical discomfort that running provided and it became incredibly therapeutic to me. It was a small amount of comfort to realize that I could control something in my life. When I ran, I could control my thoughts and have productive self-dialogue to push myself harder. When I ran, I could control my body because I could force myself to feel alive by making myself uncomfortable. The positive feelings that I had from being uncomfortable were amazing and unlocked a whole new world that I never appreciated before. But, aside from running, I was failing at everything else in my life. I failed the most around my family and I hated myself for that. My family had always been my oasis of happiness and I always treasured each day that I would pull in the driveway at home and get to see my amazing wife and three tremendous kids. My wife and kids are my world and I felt like some toxic sludge that polluted their lives. I had never been so ashamed of myself. I was the complete opposite of the partner that I wanted to be for my wife and the hero that I wanted to be for my kids. My kids were often very cautious around me as I now know that they were not happy with the person I had become.

I had lost control of myself and I only saw glimmers of normal after I would be in physically uncomfortable situations. Often when I was sucking at my home life, my family's response would be "Why don't you go for a run….". While I appreciated the permission to disappear, I also knew it was a coping mechanism for them because they were trying to survive living with someone as dysfunctional as me. They clearly did not appreciate having me around in those dark moments and probably hoped that I would come back from running as someone they could more easily tolerate.

My runs at night were somewhat reckless as I really hoped to find someone who was looking for trouble and would allow me to "successfully defend myself". It was selfish as my desire to hurt other people would only create more chaos for my family. Deep inside myself I knew this reality, but the desire to make a bad choice made me believe that I would feel so good. I was letting my dysfunctional feelings and desires get the best of me. I was trying so hard to be "normal" during the day, but I just wanted to do something to release all the rage and psychotic feelings that I was burying inside. Often the excitement to get my "high" from fantasizing a bad choice would then make me hate myself afterwards. The drastic shift from my "running high" to hating myself is what would bring me to times when I would contemplate hurting myself instead. The battle raging in my head was so overwhelming. I would think about quitting and doing something selfish, but then I would see my beautiful family and remember my blessings. I would also hear author, David Goggins reminding me to say "thank you" and push me to appreciate the calousing of my mind. I would think of so many resilient people that I had read about who chose to not give up and instead embraced the challenges. At this time, I was reading as much as I could about people who had overcome challenges. I would realize that I was not special and I was not a victim. The only victims were my family and I needed to admit that in order to be better at life, I needed to use my runs to create the productive change, and not use that time to feed the negativity.

My wife is an amazing woman, a rock who kept our family together while I was so emotionally dysfunctional. She tolerated a lot. I am forever grateful to her and I have fallen so much deeper in love with her. During all the chaos and dysfunction that my situation had created for our family, my supportive wife also found time to research a talented surgeon at NYU and convince him to find a solution to make our life better. When we met with him, he told us, " I think I can help you." Hearing those words was such a source of optimism and hope for a solution.

Thankfully, I was able to have surgery in February of 2020 at NYU to fix a hole in my auditory canal which was the source of the reverberation and echoing that I heard constantly in my head. The doctor also installed a cochlear implant in my head to assist with the tinnitus and hearing loss. The surgery allowed me to gain some control in my life and propelled me to a much better place emotionally. Living life without hearing my heartbeat in my head 24/7 and without hearing my voice echo in my head allowed me to feel more human again. My wife, once again, rose up to be my greatest hero and showed me, as always, how she loved me unconditionally. I hoped that I would return home from surgery in NYC and everything would be back to normal. Things were better and I was grateful for a return to an improved situation.

I also quickly learned the reality of mental health challenges is that once you open the door to an emotionally dark place in your mind, you can never completely close that door. I had been fighting my demons in my mind for about 2 years and I quickly realized that they are not so easy to permanently evict. I had been drowning in a sea of anxiety, psychosis and emotional dysfunction, and surgery was not going to be the only fix to managing those challenges. While dealing with the continued mental health struggles after my surgery at NYU, I realized that I had developed a great tool bag of options to positively deal with the battle that I would continue to fight within myself. I needed to continue to fight the battle within because there were no more options or quick fixes (i.e.- surgery) and I needed to be focused on getting better at life. I also never responded well to drugs, so I was very resistant to the possibility of medication as a solution.

Choosing to be physically uncomfortable was a natural repellent to anxiety (and still is) and through my experiences I have developed a mental strength to push out other crippling thoughts and emotions. I now understand the effort that it takes to push myself in ways that result in a positive outcome even though it is an uncomfortable experience. I am still amazed at how 30 minutes of movement or exercise can shift my mood 180 degrees and get my mind moving in a positive direction. Discomfort can be whatever you want it to be and whatever your threshold is. I encourage you to put forth the effort and find your "uncomfortable". I would like to be clear that I am not advocating or recommending activities that will result in physical pain or physical injury. It would be absurd to deliberately physically injure oneself because then beneficial physical activity would not be possible. Most of us know the boundaries of our comfort zone, so I am encouraging a deliberate effort to push the boundary lines and enjoy the new territory. There is pain that injures you and there is pain that changes you for the better. Learn the difference.

> "If it doesn't challenge you,
> it won't change you."
> • • • FRED DEVITO • • •

Forward Movement Choices

* Write down three physical activities that make you feel "uncomfortable":

  _____

  _____

  _____

* Commit to doing one of those activities daily for a month and note changes in how you feel.

  _____

  _____

  _____

* Write down the inner dialogue that you think is necessary to push the boundary line of your comfort zone.

  _____

  _____

  _____

* Download the 30 day challenge form at *keeponmovement.org* to track your progress.

NOTES

CHAPTER 2
Cows and Buffalo

"Nothing happens until something moves"
• • • ALBERT EINSTEIN • • •

Nick Saban is a legendary college football coach who is well-known for his career coaching at the University of Alabama. During one of his press conferences in 2023, he spoke about the importance of Nothing. He spoke about how each day we are entitled to nothing. "Nothing is acceptable but our best". Without discipline, focus and a choice to execute, we will get nothing. If we do nothing, we get nothing. However, if we do something and we provide the attention to detail, we are focused and disciplined to execute our best effort, then we get something beneficial. Nothing happens when we are willing to accept an easy and comfortable life and we are not willing to choose the path of discomfort.

The metaphor of cows and buffalo teaches us all a lesson about the ways we can choose to approach challenges and discomfort. When cows are grazing in a field and they sense a storm approaching, they will run in the opposite direction away from the storm, but it inevitably catches them. The cows will be forced to deal with the effects of the storm for a longer duration because they are moving in the same direction as the storm. However, when buffalo are grazing in a field and they sense a storm approaching, they charge directly into the path of the storm and deal with its effects for a shorter period of time because they are pushing through it to get to the other side. The learning in the metaphor is that running away from our problems like the cows can often cause the greatest amount of pain and suffering. The buffalo teaches us about confronting our problems/challenges and the benefit of working through them because it will lead to a better outcome. The buffalo also teaches us to choose our challenges by facing the problem and attacking it. Challenges are hard, so why not be like the buffalo and choose your hard and choose your uncomfortable.

Our body and our lives benefit from intentionally pushing ourselves and being uncomfortable. The discomfort makes us physically and mentally stronger to manage all of the challenges that will come before us. We also learn from managing the challenges and the discomfort that we are better suited to follow the example of the buffalo rather than the cows.

I am grateful now that I went to such a dark place emotionally because it forced me to understand and benefit from this concept. Being uncomfortable can make us all better at life and appreciate the most simple of blessings. Finding comfort in being uncomfortable has been an amazing life lesson. I know that the days that suck ultimately create space for me to be a better person. The struggle can create beauty if done with clear intention. The struggle becomes less overwhelming when we get better.

Research has shown that the anterior mid-cingulate cortex in the brain responds positively to our ability to overcome challenges and push through discomfort. It is a region of the brain that has been associated with will-power. It is an area that grows when people do things that they <u>do not want to do</u>. The anterior mid-cingulate cortex is significantly larger in people who have overcome a significant challenge. It is an area that keeps its size and increases our ability to be resilient and overcome. I would imagine that buffalo would have a larger anterior mid-cingulate cortex than cows. If you want more information on the anterior mid-cingulate cortex, I would recommend searching the Andrew Huberman podcast on YOUTube when he explains the science behind this concept.

There is a narrative that has become too common in our society that "[easy is best]{.underline}", and as a result, mediocrity has become a goal for some people. This narrative may work for some people, but those people also do not deserve the right to be disappointed when they fall short on their expectations and ambitions. Nick Saban is referring to these people in his press conference about the importance of nothing. The people who choose to embrace this mantra will never know the benefit of pushing through their challenges to reach new heights. These people will do the same thing over and over like the cows, but they will never win.

The buffalo embrace the discomfort that is created by going directly into the storm. The buffalo know that the path they choose will not be easy, but the discomfort will benefit them on the other side of the storm. The storms are inevitable and they have developed the skills to overcome the challenges ahead. The buffalo seem to accept the reality of the storm approaching and choose the discomfort to move through it. We are transformed for the better when we embrace the challenges and go at them head first. We develop a desire to attack the challenges because we know the personal benefit that comes on the other side of the storm.

The Earth has been around for approximately 4.5 billion years and shows us a lifetime of adaptation, challenges and beautiful landscapes. We need mud and rain for the flowers to grow. The thinking that we need to make things comfortable and we are so important that everyone and everything around us has to change for our benefit is selfish, and not realistic. The research and data only illustrates the benefits of overcoming challenges and pushing ourselves to be better. Managing discomfort takes great effort, which is why many people have embraced the idea that easy is best. However, effort that focuses our energy in a productive direction is life changing.

Consider this:

When water temperature is at 211 degrees, it is categorized as "hot water". When the water temperature is 212 degrees, it becomes "boiling" water. Energy and effort is needed to create "hot" water and varying levels of intensity will create varying temperatures of hot water between 100 degrees and 211 degrees. The transition from hot water to boiling water is exceptional as boiling water can be used to cook a large variety of foods, clean/disinfect surfaces, and most impressive is the fact that the steam from boiling water can even be used to power a train locomotive. Boiling water does not happen without maximum input of energy, effort and often discomfort. The same principles apply to humans as we will experience the most significant growth in life if we put forth the maximum amount of energy and effort to learn to manage and push through the discomfort.

Buffalo are like the boiling water to power the locomotive and overcome the effects of the storm. Cows are like the hot water that will slowly run from the storm and just remain "hot" with little change and most likely cool below 211 degrees as they are impacted by the sustained effects of the storm.

> "Don't wish it was easier, wish you were better.
> Don't wish for less problems, wish for more skills.
> Don't wish for less challenge, wish for more wisdom"
>
> • • • JIM ROHN • • •

Forward Movement Choices

* Go for a walk or run at least 6 days each week even when you don't want to. Be accountable and celebrate the wins for the weeks that you accomplished this goal. Write down what you are doing to hold yourself accountable.

_____

_____

* Walk or run- When you feel like you want to quit, add 3 more minutes and finish after the additional time is complete. Write down the inner dialogue that will be necessary to accomplish this:

  _____

  _____

  _____

* Push-ups, squats, planks or repetitions of any exercise- When you feel like you want to quit, do two more repetitions. Write down your feelings that you experienced when you pushed yourself beyond wanting to quit. Remind yourself of how you felt after 1 day, 1 week, 1 month and 1 year:

  1 DAY • _____

  1 WEEK • _____

  1 MONTH • _____

  1 YEAR • _____

* What is one thing you can do daily to be more like the Buffalo:

  _____

  _____

  _____

  _____

  _____

NOTES

CHAPTER 3

You Are Amazing

"The human being is born
with an inclination toward virtue"

• • • MUSONIUS RUFUS,
LECTURES, 2.7.1-2 • • •

I believe that everyone has an untapped power within them to overcome any challenge. Humans are incredibly resilient! How do we tap into that resiliency? I always wanted to be the person to adapt and overcome any situation and to never fail. However, I know that I have failed plenty of times. I feel like most of my failures were because I forgot that I was inspiring someone else. So who can we inspire? How do we show up each day? How do we show up for ourselves, and show up for others? I realized that just being someone else's cheerleader may be the inspiration to keep them from making bad choices.

I believe that most people are good, and I believe that most people are guided by honorable intentions. I believe most people want assistance in times of need, but they either struggle to ask for help, or they are too defeated to do the next hard thing. Selfishness, bad choices, hurting ourselves and laziness are all easy. Living is the hard part. How do we change the trajectory of our lives and how can we help to change the trajectory of someone else? How do we learn that it is ok to not be ok? How do we help others to realize that it is ok to not be ok?

My intention in writing this book is not to share an amazing story like I climbed Mt. Everest or went from a life of poverty to being a millionaire or that I looked death in the face and now I am achieving amazing things. I am not that person who will awe you and leave you speechless. I am a middle-aged guy who had some health challenges, then went through a really dark time; I worked really hard to overcome my demons (and continue to keep those demons away) and now I am grateful for so much in life. My intention is to share my lessons and my coping techniques, and how I manage my struggles so that it will be helpful to you. Whether someone is dealing with a life-threatening illness or someone struggles to get out of bed in the morning, the struggle is real and overcoming is necessary. We all have that power within us and we can all move forward. We may fall on our path to overcoming, and I want to encourage you to fall forward and keep moving.

I hope I can empower you! We all possess an amazing strength within ourselves to overcome huge challenges. I encourage everyone to harness that strength and keep moving forward in a positive direction.

I still battle my demons, and I also now understand that many people are fighting their own battles. I am blessed to have learned that pain always leaves a gift. The biggest lesson that I learned in my experience is that I am not special because of my challenges or demons. I am completely aware that everyone has challenges that they are dealing with every day. When we get stuck inside of ourselves we are selfish and we are thinking that we are "special". Special is not what you are! But special is what you create from overcoming your situation! It is ok to not be ok. I learned that accepting the fact that I was not ok became a turning point for me. I remember telling my wife about how really dark I was feeling back in 2020. It was the scariest thing and the most liberating feeling all at once. I was not ok at all, and that was ok. I just could not become complacent with that fact. I needed to push myself to be better and work through my challenges.

I attended Lakeland Regional High School in Wanaque, NJ. During my Junior year on the morning of May 25, 1994, an event occurred that had one of the most profound impacts on me as a young person. Around 8:30 that morning, a classmate, Amy, left our school building and went in the woods behind the school and committed suicide.

Amy was a bright girl with a great smile and a great personality. She sat directly behind me in English class, and always had a wonderful way to welcome me to class each day. I often arrived at class at the last minute and Amy was always prepared and ready for class to start. I, like so many others, had no idea what battles Amy was fighting.

I was not close friends with Amy, but the pain and sorrow that I witnessed afterwards from her friends, teachers, family and our community was like a tidal wave. I wish I had done a better job of connecting with her, but those thoughts and intentions were too late. Amy and I used to joke around in class and we would engage in small talk, but after her death, I wished I had connected with her on a deeper level.

I remember attending Amy's funeral and seeing how devastated her family and friends were. I had only attended two funerals before, but that experience of being a witness to Amy's funeral was forever imprinted in my memory. The pain and disbelief on her parents' faces was devastating. Now that I am a parent, I can only imagine the nightmare that they wanted to wake up from.

We all wondered what was going on in Amy's life that brought her to commit suicide. She was fighting a battle that we knew nothing about. Amy apparently felt that she was insignificant and had no value in the world. What could have saved her from taking her own life? Were there signs that were missed that led to Amy going to such a dark place? When Amy took her life in 1994, teen suicide was so uncommon. I remember my Dad hearing the news when he got home from work that day and he cried hysterically. Sadly, teen suicide has become all too common and many in our country seem numb to this current epidemic. One life lost to suicide is one too many.

The minister at Amy's funeral spoke about how we are all made in the perfect image of our higher power. He said, "God does not make junk". (Feel free to substitute whatever higher power that you may believe in as "God") We are all unique, and all perfect in our own way. It was tragic that Amy was not able to see that at the age of 16 and instead was carrying such a heavy burden that brought her to a very dark place. Amy was a beautiful soul who might have blossomed into an even more amazing woman. She touched the lives of so many at such a young age but she was not able to see her power or her beauty. If only Amy realized that it was <u>ok to not be ok</u>! She may have been able to get the help she needed to learn to appreciate herself. The people close to her were left wondering what they could have done to prevent this tragedy. We can do more to lift up those around us. We all struggle, but we all have the power to create a ripple effect to positively influence the lives of others.

In the Winter of 2024, my wife reminded me of an episode on the series Grey's Anatomy (season 6 episode 22) that depicted a young woman suffering from the same issues that I had dealt with. The character was suicidal and crazy, and had been diagnosed with paranoid schizophrenia. The scene began with her being restrained to a hospital bed with fuzzy cuffs on her wrists connected to the bars on her bed. When the staff removed the fuzzy cuffs and turned away to engage the girl's parents in conversation, the girl grabbed a large needle and threatened to stab herself in the chest with the hope of killing herself. She expressed that she did not want to be perceived as crazy, but yet she did feel so crazy. As the episode continued, the Doctors were arguing about her diagnosis and how to treat her. The parents provided information to the Doctors that for months the girl had been living in hell within her own head and they feared that if they left her alone for any period of time that she would kill herself. Clearly her family was suffering too. Thankfully with a little Hollywood magic and a doctor who believed that her situation was more than just schizophrenia, the doctor diagnosed her with a condition that caused her to hear every sound inside her body- Superior Canal Dehiscence Syndrome (SCDS). The girl was clearly at the end of her rope. Her parents too. Once the doctors diagnosed her and devised a plan, they brought her in for surgery. The climax was when the girl woke up and was overwhelmed by the realization that she did not hear everything going on inside her body. She kept saying, "I'm good" over and over. The doctors gave her a new opportunity in life. I could completely relate to that feeling when I woke up from my surgery and no longer heard my heartbeat, voice, steps, etc... Watching this episode reminded me of the times when I considered ending my life. I felt a constant battle within and often felt so lonely. I felt like a complete freak and knew that no one in my life could understand the crazy, paranoid, psychotic feelings that I was dealing with. I often confused the noises in my body for voices in my head. I was paranoid that people were conspiring against me and that they were causing weird noises in my head so that they could watch me struggle and act like a psycho. There were so many times that I wanted to scream and tell people about my struggle, but I feared that no one would relate to me. Mental health struggles can be so isolating. Whether you are sad, depressed, anxious or psychotic, the feelings of isolation are always there.

During many of my sleepless nights, when I was not running, I would spend time reading books and/or searching for inspiration on the internet. I wanted to find people who experienced struggle, pain, suffering, etc… and draw strength from their experience. Even though I had suicidal thoughts, I also knew that I had so much to live for. I needed to find more strength to overcome the weakness that I was feeling.

One night during the Fall of 2019, I stumbled across an inspiring human, Kevin Hines. Kevin Hines is one of five people to ever survive a suicide attempt (and make a full recovery) of jumping off the Golden Gate Bridge in San Francisco California. Kevin has transformed his life and the lives of so many through the power of his story and the way he has transformed his experience into empowering others. Kevin is honest about the isolation that he felt before attempting suicide. He shares about the bus ride to the Golden Gate Bridge that day, and how he hoped someone would see him as a person so that he would have been stopped. He presents a scene of feeling invisible on that bus. I could relate. I felt so alone even though I had such an amazing wife and kids who loved me so much. I am blessed that when a picture of suicide would start to develop in my mind, the faces of my tremendous family would appear in my mind and that would give me enough strength to step back from the edge. I understand that not everyone has a strong family support system as I do and that reality breaks my heart. If you feel that you do not have a good support system, please email me at **john@keeponmovement.org** and I will connect you with a support group or community program in your area.

For anyone struggling and needing crisis assistance, below are two resources:

✴ National Suicide Prevention Lifeline- 1-800-273 TALK(8255)
✴ 988 Lifeline (www.988lifeline.org). Call or text 988

> "The lesson: living this life until my natural end is the goal. I have learned that no matter the battle, life is always worth living"
>
> • • • KEVIN HINES *(THE ART OF BEING BROKEN - HOW STORYTELLING SAVES LIVES)* • • •

Forward Movement Choices

* Each month, write down three people in your community who inspire you. What do they do that is inspirational and what behavior or actions can you emulate:

    _____
    _____
    _____
    _____
    _____
    _____
    _____
    _____

* Read at least 1 inspirational book every six months. Write down four books that you want to read in the next two years:

    _____
    _____
    _____

* Write down how you felt and what you learned during the reading of each inspirational book.

* Write down five gifts you possess that you can share with others to be inspirational:

* Write down how you can be more aware of others who may be struggling and need support. What can you do to support others and let them know that they matter?

NOTES

CHAPTER 4

Inspire

"Always give without remembering
and always receive without forgetting"

• • • BRIAN TRACY • • •

There are so many people who have been empowered to turn tragedy or challenge into triumph. We all possess this inner strength and we can choose to engage it. "Ordinary" people who do "extraordinary" things are all around us. We are all extraordinary as we were made in the image of a higher power, "God does not make junk". I am not diving into a religious rabbit hole here, but I am saying that each of us was made to be a part of this life and contribute in some way. Whatever contribution that you choose to make can be amazing and wonderful. It can be your dedication to your family, your community, your business, your team, your country, your faith, etc. When you share your dedication and discipline with others you create a positive ripple effect. Even if you do one thing in your life that changes the trajectory of someone else's life for the better, you create momentum that moves your life and someone else's life in a wonderful direction.

My friend, Kenny Mitchell, has an organization called Operation Yellow Tape and his saying is, "There are too many of us to ever feel alone." That is such a basic concept, and yet it has such amazing power to change all of our communities for the better! There are too many of us to feel alone because we can connect with each other on some level or some way.

Kenny is a retired firefighter in Virginia who has lost fellow firefighters and first responders to suicide. His mission is to break the stigma for first responders who are supposed to compartmentalize and handle the horrific situations that they deal with inside the yellow tape of the scenes in which they respond. Our amazing first responders are expected to be brave in the kinetic moments of their job, but Kenny is working to encourage those brave people to reach out for help and process the experiences and emotions that they are feeling.

The minister at Amy's funeral in my High School left us with the final thought about being better at life in order to honor Amy's legacy. Being better to each other, reaching out to someone who may seem lonely, doing something kind for someone just because it will make someone else's day better. He encouraged us to be better at life so that we can positively influence others and so that they will know that God does not make junk. Do you have at least one person in your life (friend, colleague, neighbor, family member) that you tell each day that you love them? If not, I will connect you with someone. Email me at **john@keeponmovement.org**.

You can always empower others as you never know who you may be inspiring…

I was fortunate to participate in a community event in April 2023 at our local high school. We had lots of students and families participating throughout the day. I happened to be wearing an Operation Yellow Tape t-shirt that day with the saying on the back, "There are too many of us to ever feel alone." The event was a great success! I received a text later that evening from a parent who attended the event that day with her daughter. She sent me a picture of the back of my shirt and a note thanking me for being there. She told me that her daughter had been struggling emotionally lately and that reading the message on the back of my shirt provided her daughter with a source of strength. The simple, yet powerful message on the back of the shirt I was wearing sparked a productive conversation between the mother and daughter. Thankfully, I chose to wear that shirt to that event and the powerful message had a positive impact on someone else. Never underestimate your contribution to the ripple effect.

We have the ability to write a new chapter each day. We are the problem and the solution. Positivity, gratitude, consistency, a desire to improve, are the key ingredients for being at least 1% better each day. These ingredients allow us to embrace the struggle, be relentlessly hopeful and keep on moving forward. It does not matter if you are a high school dropout, have a GED, have a disability, a BS, an MBA or even if you are a brain surgeon, we are all capable of contributing to the ripple effect. We create what we want, both good and bad. If one person helps or inspires another person and it continues to be paid forward, then the ripple of inspiration can be massive. Let us choose to be part of the beautiful ripple effect that changes lives for the better.

We can all list many famous people who are inspirational. I was blessed to find amazing people such as Jason Redman, Kevin Hines, David Goggins, James Lawrence, Devon Still, Jake Wood, Ernie Johnson Jr, John Robinson and many others. While these people have gained notoriety and respect for their ability to overcome challenges and their professional achievements, they are still just human beings. We can learn from their mindset, attitude, emotional leadership and their choices to keep moving forward regardless of the challenges in their lives. We are all born with an ability to overcome challenges and to inspire others, or we can learn how. We can draw inspiration from the amazing people who have done a tremendous job of sharing their stories. Additionally, if we open our eyes and ears; our communities are filled with people who have made decisions to overcome everyday challenges: The single parent who lost their spouse and has two small children to raise by themself. The person born with a disability who never wants to be identified by their disability. The person who is battling a disease that will shorten their life and they just want to embrace each day. The person who chooses to sacrifice their own well-being in order to keep their community safe. The person who chooses to volunteer their time to help others just because it is the right thing to do. Many of these incredible people are all around us doing what it takes to live their best life. I challenge you to find one person each week who will inspire you to be better at life, and to be part of the ripple effect.

I am here to connect with you and encourage you to be better each day. You are a beautiful human being and you should appreciate the ability to wake up each day, take a breath and get moving. We are all resilient people if we allow ourselves to move forward. Don't forget to let your light shine each day, even if it is admitting that you are not ok.

I would like to close this chapter with a story:

FR JOHN ALDERSON, OFM FROM THE FRIARS DESK:

"Once upon a time a king and queen gave birth to a beautiful baby girl. They named her Princess Gwendolyn. She was almost perfect, except for a tiny wart on the end of her nose. It wasn't all that big, so no one paid attention to it.

As Gwendolyn grew up, the wart was still not a problem. She was too busy not only playing with her friends, but she also was a volunteer in the town soup kitchen. Every day she helped to feed the poor people in town. One day her father came home with great news. He had been to France and had arranged for Gwendolyn to marry the son of the king and queen of France.

When Gwendolyn heard the news, she nearly burst with excitement. The French prince was known to be not only strong, but very handsome as well.

Gwendolyn immediately called for the royal dressmaker to fit her for her wedding gown. The dress was beautiful, but when she stood in front of the mirror, all she noticed was that wart on the end of her nose. She became very upset, and said that the wart made her look ugly and she had to have it removed before the prince arrived. Gwendolyn then called for the palace doctor and told him to get rid of the wart. He gave her powders and ointments, but she could still see the wart. She was so angry that she threw the doctor into prison.

Then she called in the palace chef. He said that he would prepare for her a diet of fruits and vegetables and they would take away the wart. So Gwendolyn sent soldiers into town to gather up all the fruit and the vegetables. But the diet didn't work. The wart was still there. So she threw the palace chef into prison.

Then Gwendolyn called again for the royal dressmaker. He said that he would make dresses for her that would be so beautiful that no one would ever notice the wart. So Gwendolyn sent the soldiers back into town to gather up all the clothing material in the kingdom.

Even wearing these beautiful dresses, all she could see was the wart. So she threw the dressmaker into prison.

Gwendolyn was now desperate. So she called in the court magician. He said to her, "Give it away." "How?" Gwendolyn cried. "By making a law that everyone in the kingdom must paint a wart on the end of their noses. Then you will look like everyone else." So Gwendolyn sent out a royal decree that everyone in the kingdom must paint a wart on the end of their nose.

One day Gwendolyn rode into town to make sure that everyone was obeying the law. But the sight of all those people with warts on the end of their noses made her feel sick, and she headed back to the castle.

On the way home there was a terrible storm. When a flash of lightning lit up the sky, her horse jumped and she fell to the ground. She hurt her leg and all she could do was crawl to the nearest cottage.

An old man took her in and, without realizing who she was, sat her by the fire. He said that he couldn't call for the doctor because the evil Princess Gwendolyn had thrown him into prison. The old man said he couldn't make her soup, because the evil princess had taken all the vegetables to the palace. In fact, he would not even be able to put a blanket around her because the evil princess had taken all the clothing material. The old man then said, "We hate her so much that we call her the "Wart" Princess." As Gwendolyn listened to the old man, she felt ashamed of herself. She got up and ran all the way to the palace. She let the doctor and the chef and the dressmaker out of prison. She then issued a royal decree: the people could remove their warts. And she told them how sorry she was for all the ways she had hurt them. Well, the big day finally arrived. The Prince of France was coming to meet her. Gwendolyn was so ashamed of how she looked that she bowed her head and covered her face with a veil. Finally, the prince arrived. He walked up to Gwendolyn, gently lifted her face and removed the veil. When she looked up into the face of the prince, she was shocked, for right on the end of his princely nose was the biggest wart she had ever seen.

We all have our warts. But in the eyes of God we are beautiful.

God does not make junk!

Forward Movement Choices

* Focus each morning on two of the blessings in your life. Write them down each day:

  _____

  _____

* Take a 15 minute walk each day without any technology or music and just be aware of your surroundings. Write down what you saw, what you heard and how you felt:

  _____

  _____

* Tell at least one person in your life each day that you love them. Who are three people that you can say "I love you" to this week:

  _____

  _____

  _____

* What is one thing you can do each day this week to be 1% better:

  _____

  _____

NOTES

CHAPTER 5

Movement Is Anxiety's Kryptonite

"If you can't fly then run,
if you can't run then walk,
if you can't walk then crawl,
but whatever you do,
you have to keep moving forward."

• • • MLK • • •

If anxiety were a person it would be lazy and slow. It is the biggest, relentless bully in the world and it loves to make others feel small. Anxiety is not resilient and does not have any goals because it preys on others like a parasite and feeds on easy victims. Anxiety is manipulative and patient because it wants to control people. Anxiety is a huge narcissist. Just like toxic people, anxiety cannot be allowed a permanent residence in our minds.

I am not saying that people with anxiety exhibit these traits. My intention is to remind people with anxiety that they are capable of overcoming and leaving the anxiety behind them as they move forward. Anxiety is crippling and my heart goes out to everyone who is living with it. People who have not experienced the effects of anxiety have no idea how consuming it can be.

We were fortunate to go on a vacation for a week to Ocean City, NJ in July 2020. On the second to last night, we went to the boardwalk to experience all the fun that my kids had been anticipating all week. After about 15 minutes of being surrounded by big crowds, I began to have an anxiety attack. My heart began to race, my skin felt like it was crawling all over me, I felt completely powerless and disconnected from the moment and my family. Large crowds and lots of noise were huge catalysts for surges in my anxiety. In these situations, I would quickly become a person who felt like a stranger to myself and my family. My youngest daughter, Mae, could sense the dark place that I was traveling to in my mind. She quickly grabbed my hand and began to lead me towards a less crowded area off of the boardwalk. She knew that I needed to remove myself from the situation and move my body in order to return to our "fun" vacation experience.

My wife and kids were very aware of the battle going on in my mind as they were enduring the outward effects of my dysfunction for almost two years. I had been dealing with the health issues that in turn spawned my mental health issues which were significantly more damaging and dangerous than my physical health challenges. I was dealing with significant anxiety that made me feel psychotic and sometimes suicidal. My wife and kids could sense when I was not in a "good place" and they would selflessly jump in to help me. Mae, at the age of 10, had a very calming presence and she had the ability to silently pull me from the downward spiral that I was falling through that night on the boardwalk. Mae knew that taking me for a walk to a more quiet place would be the remedy and she did all of this without saying a word to me. I was a 43 year old ticking time bomb and my 10 year old daughter was the mature, calm force that made everything better.

My daughter knew to take me for a walk and get my body moving as that had become my main coping mechanism for the last two years. I had discovered that anxiety could not keep up with me if I was walking or running. Running was my primary release and the best medicine that I had discovered so far. I would run at least once a day and sometimes multiple times per day in order to deal with the battle going on in my head. Running was my therapy and it was a powerful relief from the crippling effects of the anxiety that would choke the life out of me. Although I was not able to permanently escape the grips of anxiety, I knew that anything which made me physically uncomfortable, raised my heart rate, and pulled me out of the dark place in my head was powerful medicine. Exercise became my medicine and it gave me time for lots of inner dialogue to work on getting better at life.

Many days I would come home from work and my wife could sense my anxiety levels and just give me her reassuring head nod that I should go for a run. I felt like an absolute freak with all my dysfunctional thoughts and yet my wife never made me feel that way. She just knew that I wanted to feel normal and that exercise was the best way to move in that direction. I am blessed that my wife loves me unconditionally. I am forever grateful to her for being an amazing person who tolerated me through all of my dysfunction.

Running allowed me to realize in my weakest and lowest moments, that I had a choice to either be controlled by my thoughts or work through my thoughts. I could choose to be life hardened or life weakened. I could fail by adversity or be skilled by adversity.

When I was moving my body, I experienced the powerful reality that challenges in life can be a wing or a weight. The challenge that you view as a weight will take you down to drown you or you can view the challenge as a wing that will help you fly to new heights.

It is easy to sit around and give up, easy to look the other way or avoid reality, easy to get lost in your phone, easy to be the victim. I realized that "easy" was selfish and that selfishness does not benefit anyone.

I am not discrediting the fact that some people with clinical mental health diagnoses require medication. Mental health challenges are such a debilitating experience and behavioral effects that are a result of chemical imbalances are devastating. Pharmaceuticals have their place and they provide a great benefit to those who require it. Additionally, therapy with a professional/licensed therapist can be incredibly beneficial and there are many options for in person sessions as well as online programs.

I would like to note the science behind exercise and physical movement. Myokines are a chemical that is secreted into the bloodstream during exercise from the contraction of muscles. Myokines are referred to as "Hope Molecules" as they are proteins that travel into the brain and provide an antidepressant effect. Hope molecules can enhance our overall health by improving our mood. Additionally, myokines help to reduce inflammation which provides better feelings about ourselves and allows for better muscle recovery. If we have better muscle recovery, we are more likely to feel better and stronger each time we exercise. Therefore, contracting our muscles can be equated to self-medicating our bodies with healthy chemicals that help to improve our mood, fight depression and reduce anxiety. Furthermore, we also benefit from the well-known chemicals such as dopamine, endorphins, oxytocin and serotonin. We are a living/breathing pharmacy and we have the ability to unlock these life changing chemicals by walking, dancing, running, hiking, swimming, etc… We can create such a positive and transformational impact on our brains by just exercising each day.

Physical movement develops muscle growth in our bodies. Muscle is wellness and health. The benefits of increased muscle growth are endless. Muscle growth builds our immune system, increases energy levels, increases our bodies metabolic function along with a list of other benefits. Increasing our physical health through muscle growth will only benefit our lives. Muscle fights disease, and muscle fights the aging process which makes life better. Exercise promotes glucose disposal, reduces inflammation and reduces insulin sensitivity. It promotes protein synthesis and muscle fiber regeneration. Furthermore, exercise increases BDNF levels (Brain-derived neurotrophic factor) which supports cognitive improvements as well as alleviating depression and anxiety. Exercise outdoors in the sun causes the body to release Vitamin D and increases the absorption of calcium. Exposure to the sunlight also causes the release of serotonin which is commonly referred to as the "sunshine hormone" and increases emotions of happiness and well-being. When our heart rate increases through exercise, our bodies produce adrenaline and norepinephrine, which prepares the body for physical activity to raise the heart rate and blood floor. Once we are done with the sustained increased heart rate, the body produces chemicals such as serotonin to promote relaxation and restore balance in our bodies.

Movement is life and it is an amazing therapy for the body and mind. This reality does not require an advanced degree or special training. We just need to get our bodies moving and the rest will happen by design. The 1000 mile club at San Quentin Prison is a testament to the power of movement and the life changing impact that running and physical activity can have on a person's life. The transformation that has been documented at the prison for the participants in the club is inspiring. The club began in 2005 and has grown to over 100 members. The club has become a standard for running clubs that have been formed at other prisons. In the ESPN documentary "26.2 to Life" which was made in 2022 to highlight the 1000 mile club at San Quentin, they noted that of the 45 members who have been released from prison since the club started, no one has reoffended and returned to prison. Movement is key to create momentum within ourselves physically, emotionally and spiritually.

On the most basic level, the more movement and activity that consumes your day will allow less time and space for anxiety. Being active provides a profound outlet to release the "Unwanted" from our lives and creates another thing on our daily schedule to look forward to. Movement feels good and if we can embrace the positive benefits, then we will naturally seek out opportunities to be active. We will realize the amazing power that we have to outperform the anxiety that cannot keep up with us.

Forward Movement Choices

* Dedicate at least 30 minutes per day to exercise (walking, running, weights, yoga, etc…). Hold yourself accountable to making exercise a necessary part of your daily routine and track your progress. Write down at least three activities that you are most likely to do regularly:

  _____

  _____

  _____

  _____

* Find your outlet that allows you to get away from the lazy anxiety that is following you. Write down three additional activities that you would like to try doing as part of your daily exercise (dancing, pickleball, swimming, pilates, etc.…)

  _____

  _____

  _____

* Engage your body and elevate your heart rate as often as needed. Write down how you feel and what your thoughts are before and after exercising.

NOTES

CHAPTER 6

Resilience

"Make friends with pain and
you will never be alone"

• • • KEN CHLOUBER (FOUNDER
OF THE LEADVILLE 100) • • •

Resilience cannot be found in a comfortable environment. Pain, hardships, pressure and challenges do not discriminate based upon sex, race, gender, intellect, etc… Most people want to be resilient, and we all hope that we will rise to the "challenge" when tested. However, we can't just wish for resilience and it cannot be taught in a classroom or developed by reading a book. We can be inspired by resilient people and we can study their behavior. Of course, our resilience is tested by dealing with health issues, family problems, financial challenges, etc…, but most people would not wish for that, or purposefully create these situations. Inevitably, we all will be faced with at least one or more of these challenges and we all hope to rise above them. However, we can intentionally develop resilience by choosing to challenge ourselves in ways that do not have catastrophically, life-altering experiences. Being open to choosing tasks or experiences that may result in failures that we can learn from provides space to develop resiliency.

Looking back, I think I always had a strong desire to be resilient and capable of overcoming obstacles and challenges. I often played in the woods as a child pretending to be a warrior or special operations military person who was capable of surviving in harsh conditions. I would build shelters in the woods and sharpen sticks to make weapons for hunting and protection. I would dress up in camouflage and pretend that I was forced to survive in the wilderness. Then my Mom would yell out the back door for me to come inside for dinner…. I was real tough and capable of surviving in the woods 100 feet behind my house. I did not know what resilience was then, but I pretended to.

In 6th grade I finally started to learn about resilience. I walked to and from school with a group of kids who made fun of me for being goofy and stuttering. I got punched in the face for the first time when I tried to stick up for myself after class. I did not have many friends to lean on and I realized that I was not tough. A few times I stuck up for myself but I was incredibly insecure and did not create any major change in my life. I did not know what it was like to work hard at things.

Freshman year of high school was similar to 6th grade as I did not have many friends and I was picked on for being a late bloomer. I made the soccer and basketball teams, but I did not work hard or contribute to the teams so the coaches did not have a reason to value me. I chose to try to be "all in" for Track and Field in the Spring of Freshman year until I gave up during a race and pretended to have a stomach bug. That summer, I attempted a triathlon and failed at that as well. I finally got sick of failing and committed myself to mountain bike racing and martial arts. Through mountain biking and martial arts I began to realize the basic concepts of discomfort, growth and progress. During Junior and Senior year of high school, I finally began to develop a stronger mindset and was developing my ability to be resilient.

During my Sophomore year of college, I decided that I wanted to fly planes and become an officer in the United States Marine Corps. I applied for The Platoon Leaders Class- Aviation option which would guarantee me a contract to go to flight school after graduating college. I studied harder for the test to apply to the aviation program than for any other college course. I crushed the written exam and the physical test! I was awarded a contract for the aviation program and I was to attend my first summer program at Officer Candidates School "OCS" in Quantico Virginia in 1997 which would be followed by a second program in the summer of 1998. I imagined that the experience would be tough, but I did not realize the physical and mental challenge that I needed to overcome when I arrived in Quantico. I did thrive in that environment and finally felt confident as a resilient person who had the ability to overcome challenges. I was surrounded by amazing young people who were determined to push through struggles and overcome the challenges presented before us. The life lessons that I learned during my experience at OCS about physical and mental resilience were invaluable and helped prepare me for what was to come in life.

I was amazed at how physical size and perceived strength are not a true correlation to grit and mental fortitude. Many candidates who were big and muscular would be referred to as a "PT stud" and yet I quickly learned that they did not have the mental resilience to overcome the challenges that were placed before us. Some of the smallest candidates, in terms of physical size, were the most resilient, toughest kids that I had ever met. Quitting was never an option for them and they would just put their head down and get through the evolution that they were involved in.

My experiences helped me to realize that our bodies are capable of far more than the limitations that our minds create.

Unfortunately, due to some family reasons and a change in priorities in my life, I did not move forward with my commission as an officer in the United States Marine Corps, but I learned so much about myself and the power of human resolve. The resiliency that we can all tap into is limitless if we choose to embrace the struggle and keep pushing forward. One of the greatest lessons that I learned during my time at OCS was that doing hard things and struggling can be amazing with the appropriate mindset. You can give yourself the gift of the next challenge. When you complete one challenge or overcome something, your reward is the confidence to tackle the next challenge or hardship in front of you. We owe it to ourselves to improve each day and the "easy way" is often not the most beneficial. The struggle can be beautiful!

Conversely, I have witnessed how resilience is developed through trauma. I was fortunate to work in Paterson NJ after college from 1999- 2001. Paterson is famous for East Side High School which was the basis for a movie called "Lean On Me" which highlighted the well-known principal Joe Clarke. Paterson is also famous for the boxer Rubin "Hurricane" Carter who was highlighted in a Hollywood movie made based upon his story. However, there were not a great deal of other positives when it came to talking about Paterson and as it is a very tough place for young people to grow up. The high school graduation rate in 2000 was below 60%. The gangs had a great deal of power, drug trade was huge, and organized crime controlled most aspects of the community. I worked in a program called YouthBuild which provided GED classes and construction training for young people ages 18-24. Clearly, the need for this type of program was significant and important.

I had just graduated college, I was 22 years old, and I was ready to make a difference in the world. I was the same age as many of the young people in the program, but our life experiences were vastly different. They were from the "hood" and I was from the suburbs in northern New Jersey. As a result of my upbringing, I was encouraged to go to college and most of the young people in our program had parents who struggled to care if they went to high school. All of them had lost friends to violence in their neighborhoods whereas I had never met anyone who died in a "drive-by shooting" or got stabbed to death at a party. Most of them only had a relationship with their Mom, and few Dads were around. I had very few friends who were in that situation while growing up... Even though we were the same age, they thought I must have been in my 30's because I went to college (My premature gray hair was helpful too). Most of them were not thinking much past their 20's because they were focused on daily survival and not what they were going to do for the rest of their lives. The males and females who were involved in gangs had no long-term plans at all.

I only grew up about 20 minutes away from Paterson, but my commute each day was like being teleported into another universe. I had never experienced being the "minority" and the discomfort that came with those situations was very humbling. I was raised to not concern myself with judgements about race, but about judgements based on someone's character. However, being judged based upon the color of my skin taught me so much about the resilience of the young people that I was working with, as well as their behavior. These young adults had experienced more trauma and struggles than I could have imagined. The fact that they were still alive was a huge success and testament to their resiliency. While they were not well educated in terms of schooling or academic tests, their knowledge for survival and wisdom about life was far superior to most with post-doctorate degrees. The young people in our program could have written a book on overcoming tragedy and being resilient. While they all accepted their reality, I don't think any of them would have wanted the life they had. They never would have chosen a path that began in a dark valley with such a slippery slope to climb. The level of discomfort that they experienced daily I would never wish on anyone. Yet, they were resilient enough to get up each day, put their feet on the ground and try to move in a forward direction. Resilience through trauma is incredibly powerful and something that we all need to be prepared for.

Sickness/disease, misfortune/tragedy or the situation that you are born into are not desirable choices. If you have been placed in an undesirable situation, I wish you all the strength to overcome and move forward with a resilient mind and behavior. I applaud you if you have overcome such a challenging situation. If you are struggling through an undesirable life experience, please know that I see you, I do think you are important and I do wish I could give you a hug and share some kind words with you to keep on moving forward. Few human beings would choose a life of disease, poverty, or a troublesome community.

The best way to test ourselves and develop resilience is to choose to be uncomfortable. The most simple way to be uncomfortable is to move your body, increase heart rate, lift weights, walk/run etc…. Exercise is essential as it improves your physical health, mental health and builds resiliency. Investing in yourself is the greatest gift that you can give yourself. Life gives us gifts of challenges and struggles that are inevitable. We will all be forced to overcome struggles that are self-created and/or challenges that may be outside of our control. Life is hard and pain does not discriminate. So prepare now to develop yourself and develop some tools to manage the challenges that are waiting to arrive in our lives. This is why choosing to be uncomfortable and push ourselves forward physically is so important. All the social constructs and perceptions get pushed aside because the situation becomes you vs. you. You choose to move your body. You choose to walk the extra 100 feet, the extra half mile, the extra 5 miles, etc… The number of "likes" that you receive on social media or the number of "followers" does not matter and doesn't build anything! You are winning the battle between your ears and that is your most amazing accomplishment. You choose to be better each time you go for a walk, a hike, a swim, a run, a workout, take a fitness class, etc… Eventually it no longer becomes effort as you will have a desire to push yourself forward.

I remember seeing a poster that read, "You need challenges to find your limits. You need limits to find yourself". You can choose your hard. You can choose to get outside and go for a walk when you don't feel like it. You can choose to push a friend who is struggling to go to the gym with you even though you would prefer to do something else. You can choose to do a few extra reps of an exercise in order to get stronger or better. You can choose to write down three things that you are grateful for when you really feel like life sucks and nothing is going well. You can choose to ask someone how they are doing when it is obvious that they are not in a good state of mind. You can choose to be better when it is easier to stay the same. You can choose to be a part of the ripple effect that makes our communities better when it might be easier to complain about things. You can be resilient.

There is a Jewish proverb that states: " I ask not for a lighter burden, but broader shoulders" The weight of the world is not going to get any lighter, instead your shoulders need to get stronger. We cannot control everything in our lives and there certainly is a guarantee for challenges, so building emotional resilience and "broader shoulders" will only benefit our ability to overcome. Tragedy, misfortune, pain, disease, challenges are all situations that do not discriminate based upon sex, race, family history, etc.... We cannot always change our situation, but we can always change our mindset which creates the motion to improve our situation. Dr. Henry Cloud and Dr. John Townsend are both psychologists, well known speakers and cohosts of the nationally broadcast New Life Live. They have a powerful quote that says, "We change our behavior when the pain of staying the same becomes greater than the pain of changing"

So remember:
Crawling is acceptable
Falling is acceptable
Puking is acceptable
Crying is acceptable
Pain is acceptable
Blood is acceptable
Quitting is not acceptable

Forward Movement Choices

* Continue to choose to elevate your heart-rate for at least 15 minutes a day by moving: i.e.- Walking, Running, Dancing, Swimming, Lifting Weights, etc... Then explore other options to compliment those activities: i.e.- Ice Bath, Sauna, Meditation, Walking Barefoot (grounding), Breath Work, Box Breathing, etc... Write down which activities seems to provide you the greatest benefit:

  _____
  _____
  _____
  _____
  _____

* Write down one thing you can do in your life starting tomorrow to be more resilient.

  _____
  _____
  _____
  _____

* Give yourself the gift of the next challenge. Write down a recent time when you overcame a challenge. Celebrate the win and let it guide you to continue to be an Overcomer.

NOTES

CHAPTER 7

Be Where You Are

"You look where your eyes go."
• • • DANICA PATRICK • • •

Be Where You Are. Have you seen groups of young people who are gathered together, but none of them are talking to each other because they are looking at their phones? Have you gone to a restaurant and witnessed an entire family sitting at a table together, but no one is talking because they are staring at their phones? Have you been driving in your community on a morning during the school year and watched kids with parents at their bus stops and the parent is staring at the phone and not engaging with their child? Why have we forgotten to be engaged with those who we are present with? Why are individuals more focused on the people or entertainment on the other end of their phone instead of the people they are physically with?

In April 1998, my parents and I were fortunate to meet Juliette and her father in the waiting room at the National Institute of Health (NIH) in Washington, D.C. My parents and I were at NIH because my sister was having brain surgery to remove a tumor. My sister's surgery would last almost 12 hours so we saw her off to the OR first thing in the morning and then made our way to the waiting room for a long day of trying to "keep busy". As we entered the waiting room, there was a friendly man with an English accent who greeted us. We made small talk with him for a few minutes and he said that he was at the hospital with his daughter who was there for testing. He was the only other person with us in the large waiting room that had couches, tables, games/puzzles, TV, etc… A few moments later, the door opened to the waiting room and a woman walked in with a smile that lit up the room. The man we were talking to introduced his daughter, Juliette, and she walked over to us to shake our hands and ask how we were doing. She began to ask why we were there and asked about my sister's surgery. She spoke to us for about 15 minutes about where we lived, what we were doing in life, etc… Shortly after, a nurse came into the room and asked Juliette to come with her. When Juliette left the room, my mom asked her father if he would share about Juliette's situation and how she was doing. Her father began to tell us about her rare disease and how she was one of the few "older" living persons with her type of disease so there was a lot of interest to study her situation. I would never have imagined that my initial interaction with someone in Juliette's situation would have been so pleasant and self-less. I would have expected her to be preoccupied and nervous or overwhelmed. I would have thought she would be distant and distracted given her busy day ahead of tests and procedures. However, her dad said that she is the most amazing, resilient person that he has ever met. How could someone with such a rare disease who knew that she likely did not have long to live, be so present and engaged with strangers like my parents and me? Juliette was entitled to pull the health card and just be miserable and throw a pity party, but she was the complete opposite. She chose to live each moment to the fullest and she chose to focus on experiencing life for all that it is. Juliette chose to give up her time with her friends and family to travel to the US multiple times a year for testing so that she could provide insight to researchers working on her rare disease to develop treatments to save others dealing with the same disease.

Juliette was a woman who had an amazing energy and a warm smile that made anyone who met her feel an instant connection. Juliette would sit with you and speak to you as if you were the only person who mattered at that moment. Juliette would never focus any attention on the fact that she was living with a rare, fatal disease that only impacts one in 250,000 people. Julliete had every reason to be negative and angry about her situation, but instead she chose to focus on engaging others and living in each moment.

Juliette returned to the waiting room mid-morning and sat down at the table with my mom and I as we were working on a large puzzle. She asked if she could jump in and help us with it. While working on the puzzle together, she was sharing with us about life in the UK and she was asking more about my sister and where my parents were from in NJ. She was asking me about college and my life plans. Juliette was one of the purest examples of being where you are. We were fortunate to have several other time blocks with Juliette throughout the day and we were blessed with her bright energy while dealing with the stress of knowing that my sister was having brain surgery. Meeting Juliette also provided us with perspective that life challenges do not discriminate and that my sister was fortunate to be dealing with a situation that had many positive options. More than 25 years later, I realize that meeting Juliette left a permanent impact in my life and a reminder that we all need to be present and grateful for what we do have. Reminding ourselves of the reality that "everyone is dealing with something difficult and/or tragic" allows us to be better at life. Oftentimes people are dealing with issues that are much more challenging than ours and we need to focus on being considerate to others and be more self-less. Be with the people who you are with. Our world needs more Juliettes!

If your eyes are on your phone, that will guide you into the digital world. If your eyes are on those that you are with then you will engage with them and benefit from the human connection. There is a saying that reminds us to **be thankful for today- yesterday is history, tomorrow is a mystery and today is a gift that is why they call it the "present".** There are two days of the year that nothing can be done- Yesterday and Tomorrow.

The other lesson to take from Danica Patrick's quote, "You look where your eyes go", is that looking back does you no good. Looking at others on social media and worrying about them and what they are doing does not benefit you either. It certainly will not make you present where you are. This concept applies to our thoughts, feelings, intentions, etc… Where your mind goes is where you go. A person cannot create a productive life if they focus on negative/paralyzing thoughts. If you tell yourself that you feel sad, or you suck at something, then you will always feel sad and suck at things.

Be where you are. Whether we are struggling or content, happy or sad, angry or satisfied, living your best life or dragging yourself out of bed each morning, you are awesome because you are where you are and you have the power to be better each day.

It is not awesome to compare yourself to what others do, or have or to believe that your perceptions of others are 100% true. You are not able to see or understand all the background of each persons' life. You also do not know what false truths may be shown on social media and often a false facade is what is being presented. Perspective is everything.

* One day, a rich dad from California took his son on a trip to Mexico to experience how poor people live. They spent time on the farm of a poor family and got to experience their daily routine. After a few days in Mexico, the father felt like he had done a great job showing his son how poor people lived. On the way back to California, the dad asked his son, "What did you learn from this trip?". The son said, "We have one dog and they have four. We have a pool and they have a river. We have tube-lights and they have stars. We buy food and they grow their food. We have walls to protect us and they have friends to protect them. We have television and they spend time with family and relatives." The son paused and looked at his dad and said, "Thanks dad for showing me how poor we are."

We should all think about our perspective and our perceptions about life. How has our ability diminished to be considerate, compassionate, display empathy and just be kind to others? Why are we accepting this negative impact on all of us? How do we increase our desire to be better people each day? The son in the story above reminds all of us about what it means to Be Where You Are.

Presently, we are living in a time where we are all so digitally distracted that we struggle to even acknowledge the level of dysfunction that exists all around us. We are all contributing to the dysfunction as we are all guilty because the addiction to technology does not discriminate. We have all been guilty of one or more of the following:

* The mom/dad at the bus stop who chooses to answer emails or scroll through his/her phone instead of engaging with their child as they start their day at school.
* The mom/dad who is scrolling through their phone while the child is asking for assistance with homework.
* The family or couple sitting at dinner and staring at phones instead of connecting about their day.
* The group of kids gathered together who are not talking because their heads are buried in a device.
* The child who chooses to binge watch 5 episodes of a "reality" show instead of going outside to create their own "reality".

* Asking someone a question multiple times because they were distracted by their phone the first time you asked them.
* Having someone tell you to "wait a minute" because they "just need to text/snap/ or whatever to their friend", as if the person on the other end of the phone is more important than you.
* Insert additional examples you are guilty of….

You are awesome because you have the power to live your own life and not just watch others live theirs. It is not awesome to let yourself believe negative thoughts about what you cannot do and what your perceived limitations are. You are awesome because you have the power to embrace all the pain and misery that you may be experiencing and invest in yourself to blossom into the beautiful creature that you were always meant to be. You owe it to yourself to stop "shoulding" on yourself- I should have done this or that…. You owe it to yourself to push forward when you feel the tendency to put yourself down. You owe it to yourself to be where you are and love yourself for it. Until we love ourselves for where we are and we are accountable for all of it, we cannot move forward on to great new things. We need that self-acceptance and accountability as a foundation to move on to the next wonderful chapter of success and happiness.

"Your time is limited, so don't waste it living someone else's life. Don't be trapped by dogma- which is living with the results of other people's thinking. Don't let the noise of others' opinions drown out your own inner voice. And most important, have the courage to follow your heart and intuition. They somehow already know what you truly want to become."

• • • STEVE JOBS • • •

Forward Movement Choices

✳ Go for a 20 minute walk each day without your phone. Write down any changes to your ability to be more present with those around you after your walk.

_____

_____

_____

_____

* Make a Family rule- No phones at the dinner table. List discussion topics that you would like to cover with your family:

　_____

　_____

　_____

　_____

　_____

* Share at least three compliments a day with someone you know. List off the first five people that you would like to do this for:

　_____

　_____

　_____

　_____

　_____

* Write down five ways you can be more present with family and friends.

　_____

　_____

　_____

　_____

　_____

NOTES

CHAPTER 8

Be Grateful

> "He is a wise man who does not grieve for the things which he has not, but rejoices for those which he has."
>
> • • • EPICTETUS • • •

On Saint Patrick's Day 2019, I was trying to get some things done at my house as I was going to have my first surgery three weeks later and I knew that I would not be able to get housework done for a little while. My wife had been asking me for a long time to build shelves in an area of our kitchen where we had some wasted space and having shelves there would make her happy. Given the fact that I am a carpenter and can easily build the shelves, I would be dumb to delay her happiness any longer and I should just install the shelves so that she can enjoy having the additional storage. I had my tools and saw set up in the garage and I was hustling to get them complete. As I was ripping material on the table saw, I reached over to the side of the saw to grab the "push stick" to finish cutting the material safely so that my fingers would not be near the blade. Unfortunately, as I was grabbing the push stick the material got pulled through the spinning blade and then it happened; my hand bounced off the blade. Immediately, I felt a burning on my left pointer finger and my glove was covered in blood. As I took my glove off, my finger looked like a sausage that had been cut wide open. My wife and son were out running errands and I was so afraid to add one more thing for my wife to deal with so I did not call her right away. My two daughters were playing inside the house and I did not want to scare them with my bloody hand so I did not disturb them either. I wrapped my hand in a towel and called my brother in law to ask him to give me a ride to the hospital.

As I paced around the room in the ER at the hospital, my anxiety surged and my mind was racing in a thousand directions. I was afraid to tell my wife that I just complicated our lives even more, I was afraid that I would not be able to have my surgery which had been scheduled for several months and I was afraid that I permanently disabled myself by cutting off my finger. Fortunately, I had only partially cut through my bone and only slightly damaged my tendon. Given the fact that I am like a starfish, I cut off part of my right thumb about 15 years earlier and most of it grew back, I knew that I would recover. I had less than three weeks until my surgery and I needed to heal enough so that the surgeon would clear me for the procedure.

As my finger began to heal, I realized that this was preparation for the next chapter. I was going through the experience with my finger so that I would appreciate life and be thankful for my blessings. I needed to prepare for the next obstacle ahead so I gave myself the gift of the next challenge. The perspective that I would gain from my damaged finger would be necessary so that I could manage the challenges and pain that I was about to experience.

I have a history for being the guy who is blessed with the small percentage of complications and rare health scares that kick you in the ass and test your fortitude.

As I mentioned earlier, I cut off part of the thumb with a circular saw back in 2004 shortly after starting my construction business. Then in 2010, I spent a week in the hospital with several devastating tick diseases where my platelets dropped to dangerous levels. I also had complications from nasal/sinus surgery where I was the 1% to get an infection post-op and I had to be cut back open without anesthesia so they could vacuum the infection out of my nose. I am not saying that these experiences make me special, but I am acknowledging that I am grateful for the learning and perspective gained as a result. Each time that I found my health compromised, I gained a stronger gratitude for life and the many blessings that I had. I also learned to find friendship in pain and that became a huge source of strength for the very dark time in my life. All of my life experiences were preparing me for a sense of gratitude that would be necessary for me to live. Gratitude leads to positivity and relentless positivity creates a revolving door of gratitude.

The lessons in gratitude finally sunk in for me a few days after my surgery in April 2019. When I woke from the anesthesia I regretted the whole thing. I felt like I had been hit by a truck and completely screwed up my life. I was laying in the bed at the ICU about 3 days after my surgery. I was deaf on my left side, my tinnitus was still awful, I had no balance because they cut my balance nerve (they do that on purpose) and I felt weak and useless. After a few days, I realized that I would improve and I needed to push forward. I had seen enough people come into the ICU who were in much worse condition than I and many of them permanently impacted in drastic ways from their health issues. I realized that I needed to be grateful for all that I had. I realized that everyone has stuff going on in their lives and there is always someone worse off than I so I did not deserve to be the "victim". Being the victim was selfish and the battle against being a selfish victim had been ongoing for me.

Positivity is a natural repellant for negativity. Negativity and anxiety are from the same family as they both would be lazy, slow and useless people. Negativity is an incredibly contagious emotion and spreads easily. For every opportunity that we have to be sad and negative, there are just as many opportunities to be positive. My kids think I am annoying because I always tell them that attitude is energy and energy is attitude. I am a firm believer that life can change when you choose positivity. Some days suck and you feel like a complete failure. However, we are blessed with a new tomorrow. Every trigger is an invitation to grow. Focus on each day as if it is the first day of the rest of your life. We can reset ourselves each day and be a champion of tomorrow. Furthermore, gratitude and any negative attitude cannot exist at the same time within our bodies. Gratitude can change any emotional state.

I began to research more about gratitude and the powerful impact on the body and our neurochemistry. I learned more specifically about using a gratitude list and the tremendous changes that result. Multiple times each day (as often as needed) I experienced the instant effects of reciting my gratitude list and feeling the amazing reduction in anxiety and stress. My gratitude list has been one of my greatest medicines for managing anxiety and other negative thoughts in my head. Feelings of gratitude regulate the cortisol production in our brains and trigger the release of neurotransmitters and hormones associated with happiness. Dopamine and serotonin are released and can instantly change our moods and mindset.

On December 25, 2019, my kids gave me one of the most functional Christmas presents ever, a book called UNFU*K YOURSELF by Gary John Bishop. Reading the book was a life-changing experience. I am so proud of my kids' honesty and loving support to turn their frustration with me into something productive by giving me a resource to be better. Their honesty was something that inspired me instantly. Three of the most important people in my life were telling me that only I could unfu*k myself. I created the reality that I was existing in and only I could change that reality. I have always said that my kids are my inspiration and my "why", but I had completely lost sight of that reality when I allowed myself to get stuck in my head. I am grateful that my kids loved me enough to be my cheerleaders and were not afraid to offend me by being honest with me about the situation. They sent me a message loud and clear that was safe, loving and supportive. Ironically, the second part of the title of the book is "Get out of our head and into your life". Getting out of my head and back into my kids' lives was essential.

The book, UNFU*K YOURSELF, was such a great lesson in life as it provides the most basic concept that we should be grateful for the ability to wake up each day and create whatever we want. All the bullshit and details do not matter as much as the fact that we are beautiful human beings with the ability to wake up each day. If we embrace that simple fact, then we are open to all the great things in our lives that we should be grateful for. I am not just talking about family, money, perceived success and employment. I am talking about the sun, the rain, the warmth, the cold, the ability to feel, see, smell and experience life. I have learned to be grateful for the good and the bad. Every great moment is an opportunity to appreciate life just as every trigger in our lives is an invitation to grow. My kids knew that I was being tested in life and that I needed a vehicle to support these character building experiences. I wanted to be grateful, but I was stuck in my head. I needed a reminder to unfu*k myself and that Christmas present from them was a great reminder that I was capable of being better and living a life with more gratitude.

My daily gratitude list has become my first line of defense against negative thoughts that attempt to reside in my head. When I experience a major anxiety attack and I want to jump out of my skin, I begin to recite my gratitude list in my head and it fuels me to resist the negative feelings and my heart rate begins to calm. I am realistic. This strategy is not 100% perfect, but it provides amazing assistance and always opens a door to a better place. Research has shown that gratitude journaling is proven to increase self-worth, strengthen relationships, improve perspective, increase optimism and improve sleep quality. Gratitude journaling will only enhance our lives and there is no data that there is a negative outcome.

I still get sad and have weak moments because I am human. Anxiety attacks are still a reality for me and I am forced to overcome them at times. No one is immune to negative feelings. I encourage anyone to put forth effort into developing a gratitude list and making a concerted effort to find more grace in your life. Our world is filled with blessings. Don't forget that we all can be a name on someone else's gratitude list.

Opportunities are all around us and everything happens the right way, we just don't always want to see it or believe it. We need to see things from an opportunity stand point and not from a "loss" mindset. Everything happens for a reason.

"Go without a coat when it's cold; find out what cold is. Go hungry; keep your existence lean. Wear away the fat, get down to the lean tissue and see what it's all about. The only time you define your character is when you go without. In times of hardship, you find out what you're made of and what you're capable of. If you're never tested, you'll never define your character."

• • • HENRY ROLLINS • • •

Forward Movement Choices

* Spend 2 minutes a day writing in a gratitude journal. Write your first journal entry below (use the notes section if you need more space):

_____

_____

_____

_____

_____

_____

_____

* Meditate for 3 minutes a day and focus on specific people and/or actions that will increase your gratitude. Write down key words or thoughts that you found most powerful during meditation:

  _____

  _____

  _____

  _____

* Write down three feelings/emotions that you feel after meditating and focusing on positive inner dialogue.

  _____

  _____

  _____

  _____

* Write a thank you note to someone expressing your appreciation for them. Do this at least once per month. Write down the names of the first three people that you would like to do this for:

  _____

  _____

  _____

  _____

  _____

NOTES

CHAPTER 9

Flip The Switch/ Re-Write Your Story

••• TALE OF TWO WOLVES •••

An old Chrokee told his grandson, "My son, there is a battle between two wolves inside us all. One is Evil. It is anger, jealousy, greed, resentment, inferiority, lies and ego. The other is Good. It is joy, peace, love, hope, humility, kindness, empathy and truth."

The boy thought about it and asked, "Grandfather, which wolf wins?" The old man quietly replied, "The one you feed."

On October 30, 2021, I went out early in the morning for a typical Saturday morning run. The sun was rising, the leaves were falling, the birds were chirping and I felt an amazing wave of power wrap around my brain. That Saturday morning run became an incredibly transformational day for me. I felt a shift in my soul. I was finally ready to let go of my dysfunctional thoughts and behaviors that served as a crutch. I would finally embrace my intentional gratitude 100%. I had wanted to feel this shift for quite a while, but I had not worked hard enough to be better at life. It had been two and half years since I first started my journey overcoming the darkest time of my life. I finally felt capable and confident in myself that I could let go of the past and see my experiences with gratitude. I had been holding onto such resentment for the darkness that I experienced and I could not completely move forward. I needed to be all in on my gratitude for the journey of the last two and half years and truly appreciate the experience. The feelings of gratitude that I experienced during that run were amazing. I felt like a moth leaving the cocoon and emerging with a new sense of life and purpose. I am no butterfly, but I certainly had a cocoon around me that was holding all of my undesirable behaviors.

I felt like the grandson of the Cherokee who finally realized which wolf I needed to feed. The gratitude that I wanted to feel for all the challenges and dark times was finally present. I was grateful for all of it. I knew that this was not an ending, instead it was a new beginning. I broke through a barrier in myself that had been so solid for too long. I would always tell myself each day that it was the first day of the rest of my life, but that day on October 30, 2021, I finally was able to manifest those words into feelings. I still tell myself each day that it is a great day to be alive and that it is the first day of the rest of my life, but it truly felt that way when I finished my run. I have learned that there is a big difference between saying something and feeling something. It feels so good to know the difference. Some days it is a monumental struggle to say it and feel it as I would be a hypocrite if I was not honest about that reality. However, I know inside that I do have the power to feel it and create it. Some days really feel like I am getting the crap beat out of me by Mike Tyson, but I know that I am strong enough to make it to the next day.

I realized that a huge part of this transformation was acknowledging that I was both the problem and the solution. This is a very difficult pill to swallow. I thought that I would be better at life because I overcame some challenges. However, I needed to realize that the act of overcoming did not make me special. I had to be accountable for myself. I was the problem and only I could fix it. Fully embracing and appreciating the source of all my anxiety and dysfunction was the solution. I worked so hard to be grateful for a while, but I needed to focus on the solutions that I just had to resolve inside of me. I needed to change my inner dialogue and to acknowledge that I am the problem and the solution.

I still stumble over myself mostly by getting in my own way. I still feel the negative messages trying to work their way into my mind. In fact, as I am writing this on September 15, 2024 (my 23rd wedding anniversary), I just finished an uncomfortable exercise routine that I needed to do in order for me to make today a great day for my wife! Exercising in such a way that it provides me discomfort now brings me such peace.

As Andrew Huberman was quoted on a podcast in saying the following two statements: **"The mind follows the body" & "Use the body to create change in the mind."** I now know the power that my body has to change and overcome the dysfunction in my mind. I rely upon it as a natural medicine that really does make everyday a great day to be alive.

I also know that it is ok to not be ok. We can train our minds to accept and transform the negativity into something beautiful. I think it can be possible to permanently evict the problematic messages from our brains, and we can do it with gratitude, forward movement, and knowing that we all possess an amazing power to take control of our lives.

As we learn from the cows and buffalos, we can choose our hard. Life is not about waiting for the storm to pass, but for learning to dance in the rain. Everyone suffers as pain and heartache are a guarantee in life. We do not need to be defined by our challenges or our past. Our challenges force us to become stronger so that we can have the strength to break free from our struggles and challenges. We become stronger through adversity. I learned that struggling and challenging is an opportunity to become stronger in order to move closer to the person that I am ultimately meant to be. Avoiding the struggle robs us of the time and experience to develop ourselves and grow stronger. The challenges and struggles shape us so that we can move to better places and situations because we are stronger and more capable.

I want to acknowledge that all of this is hard and it can be an exhausting process to transform your life. It is easy to choose to just accept things in our lives that are not ideal or that may be dysfunctional. Acceptance of the "status quo" in our lives needs to be a habit to eliminate. Eliminating poor habits in our lives is hard and often the thought of doing what is necessary to create the change is overwhelming. I would be a hypocrite if I did not acknowledge that challenge. The process for change is also a long journey that can be exhausting. I want you to use the tools that I have shared in order to embrace the struggle.

Everything that I have written about is hard. I want to distinguish that the hard part is not the action. The hard part is starting. Whether you are starting your process on the first day or the 1000th day, starting each day is hard. This is why I encourage you to focus on positive self-dialogue and find an addiction to positivity. I have worked to fill my life with inspiration and positivity through reading, podcasts, quotes, etc… For the last five years I have overdosed on as much positivity and as much inspiration as possible so that I can embrace all of the hard times and struggles. Once the action begins, then we create momentum. The satisfaction that we gain from forcing ourselves to do things that we know will benefit us is what gives us momentum. Our anterior mid-cingulate cortex also grows when we force ourselves to do those things and then we become better at pushing ourselves through challenges. This momentum carries us to finish each day and prepare for the next.

Once we flip the switch and do not let ourselves be controlled by our struggles, then we have the beautiful opportunity to give ourselves to others. Spread some love! Research has shown that love can have significant positive impacts on our physical and mental health. Feeling loved can help reduce stress and promote healthier lifestyle choices. Studies have shown that love reduces blood pressure and can reduce physical pain. Love will always improve mental health as social isolation and loneliness have detrimental effects on our mental health. It feels good to love others. Sharing a smile is beautiful. I have learned that the energy we put out is what reflects back at us. After I flipped the switch in October 2021 and found true gratitude, I also began to embrace the power of positivity. I feel like my life has become much deeper and I have felt a "fullness" much greater than ever before. My ability to appreciate good people and my desire to be a cheerleader for others has grown significantly.

Mark Twain is credited with saying, "The two most important days in your life are the day you are born and the day you find out why." Once I learned to flip the switch, I was empowered to help others who may be going through mental health and physical health challenges. The sense of empathy that I have gained through this experience has been massive. Understanding that health challenges (both physically and mentally) are overwhelming and those challenges have a profound impact on the family as a whole. I have been inspired by so many people and in some cases it seemed like their message was meant specifically for me. I have realized that I can be someone else's inspiration or at least I can bring some love into their day.

"Everybody can be great because anybody can serve. You don't have to have a college degree to serve. You don't have to make your subject and verb agree to serve. You don't have to know about Plato and Aristotle to serve. You don't have to know Einstein's Theory of Relativity to serve. You don't need to know the Second Theory of Thermodynamics and Physics to serve. You only need a heart full of grace. A soul generated by love."- Martin Luther King, Jr.

If you only get one thing from the pages in this book, I want it to be a call to action to move your body. The key ingredient to confronting challenges, overcoming and growing is moving your body so that your mind, your spirit, your emotions and your life can be better. Even when things suck, a body moving forward is better than a body stuck in one location.

> "The mark of any man, woman, or organization is not found in their past, but how they overcome adversity and build their future"
>
> • • • JASON REDMAN • • •

Forward Movement Choices

* Get started on something. Find something simple and small to start with and then build upon that. Create discipline and consistency in your actions. Write down what you are doing to get started on this week and hold yourself accountable to be consistent:

  _____

  _____

* Commit to moving your body: The type of and size of movement is not important. The consistency and desire to increase the amount of movement over time is what is important. We all move at different paces, but the consistency and discipline to keep moving forward is essential. How are you going to hold yourself accountable?

  _____

  _____

  _____

* Get Started and Never Stop! Email me at **john@keeponmovement.org** if you need anything. I believe in you and I am sure that others believe in you. You need to believe in yourself and you need to know that you are the solution. What one change will you make each day to remind yourself that you have the power to be an Overcomer?

NOTES

RE-WRITING YOUR STORY

"Your current situation is
not your final destination.
The best is yet to come."

• • • ZIG ZIGLAR • • •

* Physical Abilities:
* Exercise/physical activity:
  * Hope Molecules- Myokines- Proteins released when muscles contract. Natural chemicals improve our mood, reduce inflammation and reduce anxiety.
  * Humans benefit from the well known chemicals such as dopamine, endorphins, oxytocin and serotonin.
  * Discipline is the best form of self love- Denying yourself the instant gratification for the long term benefits of hard work
  * Be uncomfortable: Give yourself the gift of the next challenge

- Increasing the size of the anterior cingulate cortex by overcoming the challenges
* Knowing all of this stuff leads into the benefits of positivity
* Positivity:
  - Brain works 31% better when in a positive frame of mind (exercise gets you there)
  - Mirror Neurons- share a smile & receive a smile
  - Relentless positivity builds an armor or calousing as David Goggins would say
* Gratitude:
  - Releases positive neurotransmitters- serotonin, dopamine, oxytocin
  - Reduces Cortisol (stress hormone)
  - Engages the parasympathetic nervous system when we are grateful (nerves that help us to relax)
  - Focusing on what we are grateful for lessens our focus on the frustration and dysfunction
  - Being grateful for the dysfunction and challenges as they allow us to become better people
  - Don't forget that you are amazing with a tremendous power to overcome

- Flip The Switch:
  - **Build up enough strength within so that you can flip the switch and live the life that you have been telling yourself that you wanted*
- Human Connection:
  - Hugs are medicine
  - Honesty with loved ones is powerful medicine.
  - Find ways to not feel alone and not feel like an outcast - Realize that there are others out there
  - Finding ways to serve others and lift up others
  - Get out of your head

"Growth is painful. Change is painful. But nothing is as painful as staying stuck somewhere you don't belong."

• • • MANDY HALE • • •

RESOURCES

RECOMMENDED READING:

- *Can't Hurt Me* • David Goggins
- *Comfortable With Uncertainty* • Pema Chodron
- *Get Off Your Knees* • John Robinson
- *Hero On A MIssion* • Donald Miller
- *Iron Cowboy* • James Lawrence
- *Make Your Bed* • Admiral William H. McRaven
- *Man's Search For Meaning* • Viktor E. Frankl
- *Never Finished* • David Goggins
- *Once A Warrior* • Jake Wood
- *Overcome* • Jason Redman
- *Running Is My Therapy* • Scott Douglas
- *Soul Friends* • Stephen Cope
- *Still In The Game* • Devon Still
- *The Art of Being Broken: How Storytelling Saves Lives* • Kevin W. Hines

- *The Daily Stoic* • Ryan Holiday
- *The Dharma In Difficult Times* • Stephen Cope
- *The Obstacle Is The Way* • Ryan Holiday
- *The Trident* • Jason Redman
- *Through the Eyes of One?* • Kevin W. Hines
- *Transformed* • Remi Adeleke
- *Unfu*k Yourself* • Gary John Bishop
- *Unscripted* • Ernie Johnson Jr.

RECOMMENDED PODCASTS:

- *Huberman Lab Podcast* • Dr. Andrew Huberman
- *Impact Theory Podcast* • Tom Bilyeu
- *Mel Robbins Podcast* • Mel Robbins
- *Modern Wisdom Podcast* • Chris Williamson
- *Operation Yellow Tape Podcast* • Kenny Mitchell Jr.
- *Rich Roll Podcast* • Rich Roll
- *School Of Greatness Podcast* • Lewis Howes
- *Sean Ryan Show* • Sean Ryan

JOIN THE MOVEMENT:

www.keeponmovement.org

- Apparel
- Donations
- Challenges
- keeponmovementorg

NOTES